THE TINY PERFECT
DINOSAUR
BOOK ONE

PRESENTING LEPTOCERATOPS

BY **JOHN ACORN** WITH **DALE RUSSELL** ILLUSTRATED BY **ELY KISH**

A SOMERVILLE HOUSE BOOK

ANDREWS AND **McMEEL**

A UNIVERSAL PRESS SYNDICATE COMPANY • KANSAS CITY

Contents

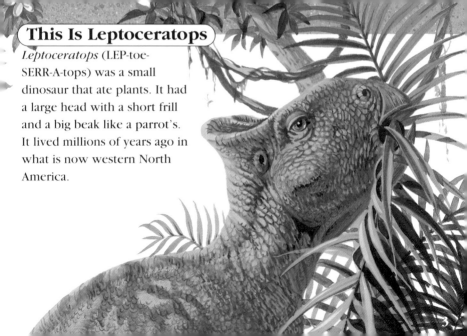

This Is Leptoceratops

Leptoceratops (LEP-toe-SERR-A-tops) was a small dinosaur that ate plants. It had a large head with a short frill and a big beak like a parrot's. It lived millions of years ago in what is now western North America.

Amazing Dinosaurs

A long time ago, dinosaurs were the largest animals on earth. But now they are all gone. The last dinosaur died long before any of us were born.

Dinosaurs were reptiles, like lizards and snakes. Although some were as small as a pigeon, and some were the size of a bus, they all were bare-skinned, they all laid eggs, and they all walked erect.

Unlike dragons, which are imaginary, dinosaurs really lived on earth. But like dragons, some were quite terrifying. (The name *dinosaur* means terrible lizard.)

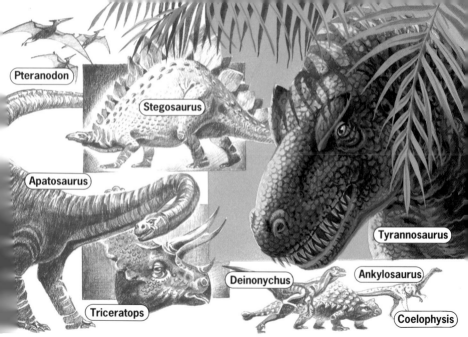

Pteranodon

Stegosaurus

Apatosaurus

Tyrannosaurus

Triceratops

Deinonychus

Ankylosaurus

Coelophysis

Leptoceratops was not very large for a dinosaur. From the tip of its tail to the end of its beak, it was only about six feet (two meters) long. If you could put one on a scale, it would probably weigh about as much as an average person.

We don't know what color *Leptoceratops* was. Maybe it was the color of the plants. Then meat-eating dinosaurs would have had a hard time seeing it.

Fossils

Fossils are made when an egg or a footprint or a dead animal is covered by mud or sand. Usually only the bones and teeth of animals turn to rock and become fossils. The softer parts, like skin and muscles and stomach, decay and disappear. Sometimes scavenger animals eat the meat off the bones before the bones turn into fossils.

Leptoceratops's back legs were longer than its front ones. On each front foot, it had five toes. On each back foot, it had four toes. At the end of each toe was a thick toenail to protect it.

A dinosaur dies.

e bones are covered up.

The bones turn to rock.

The fossils of the bones are discovered.

Studying Fossils

Everything we know about dinosaurs comes from fossils. People who study fossils are called paleontologists (PAY-lee-on-TAW-lo-jists). They find the fossils, dig them out of the ground, then put the fossils back together again. By looking at the fossils, paleontologists try to guess what the dinosaurs looked like.

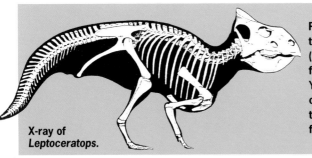

X-ray of *Leptoceratops.*

Put together the bones that came with this book. (See the back of the box for exact instructions.) You will have a skeleton of *Leptoceratops,* just like the fossil bones that were found in Alberta, Canada.

In 1910 a paleontologist named Barnum Brown was floating down the Red Deer River on a scow — a big boat with a tent on top. When he stopped the boat near a place called Rumsey, in Alberta, Canada, he found two skeletons of *Leptoceratops* near the river. He was sorry to see that cows had been walking on the fossils. Many of the bones in the skeletons had been destroyed.

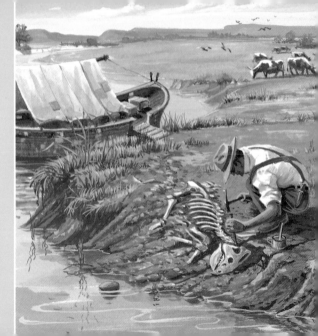

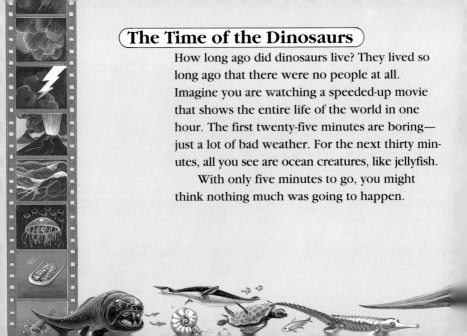

The Time of the Dinosaurs

How long ago did dinosaurs live? They lived so long ago that there were no people at all. Imagine you are watching a speeded-up movie that shows the entire life of the world in one hour. The first twenty-five minutes are boring—just a lot of bad weather. For the next thirty minutes, all you see are ocean creatures, like jellyfish.

With only five minutes to go, you might think nothing much was going to happen.

Suddenly, four minutes before the end of the movie, the first land animals appear. The first dinosaurs show up with two and a quarter minutes to go. After a two-second pause, a lot of big mammals appear. Finally, during the last sixth of a second, the first people show up.

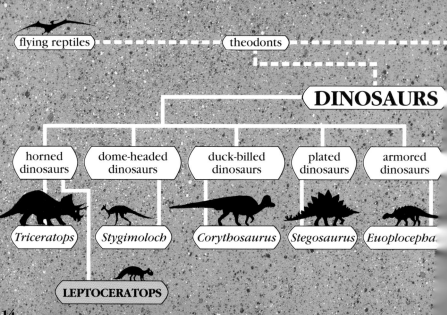

flying reptiles — theodonts

DINOSAURS

| horned dinosaurs | dome-headed dinosaurs | duck-billed dinosaurs | plated dinosaurs | armored dinosaurs |

Triceratops *Stygimoloch* *Corythosaurus* *Stegosaurus* *Euoplocepha*

LEPTOCERATOPS

14

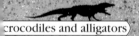

crocodiles and alligators

Family Tree

Paleontologists classify dinosaurs in many different groups. Here are some of the famous dinosaurs, and the groups they belong in.

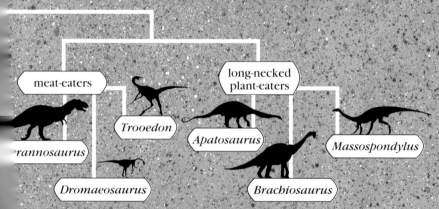

meat-eaters

Trooedon

long-necked plant-eaters

Apatosaurus

Massospondylus

rannosaurus

Dromaeosaurus

Brachiosaurus

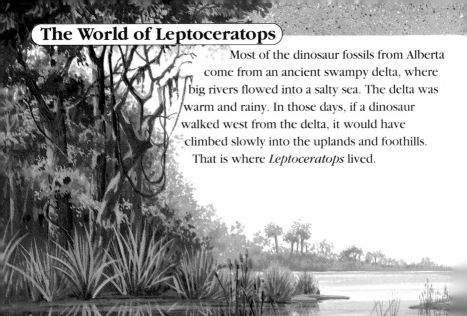

The World of Leptoceratops

Most of the dinosaur fossils from Alberta come from an ancient swampy delta, where big rivers flowed into a salty sea. The delta was warm and rainy. In those days, if a dinosaur walked west from the delta, it would have climbed slowly into the uplands and foothills. That is where *Leptoceratops* lived.

Paleontologists think the biggest types of horned dinosaurs, like the *Triceratops* (Try-SERR-A-tops), lived in swampy country and lowlands. They had teeth for slicing plants, and they probably ate mostly leaves. The smaller types of horned dinosaurs, like *Leptoceratops*, lived in the uplands. These places didn't have as many plants growing in them as the swampy jungles and the delta did.

Solid green shows the world 65 million years ago. The line shows the map today.

The delta and the uplands.

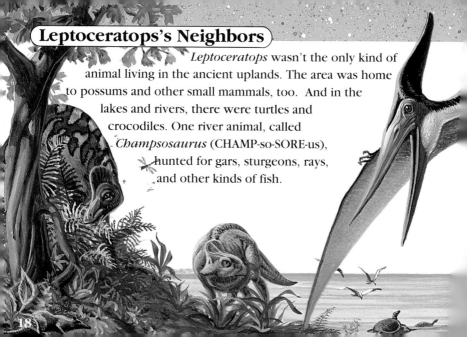

Leptoceratops's Neighbors

Leptoceratops wasn't the only kind of animal living in the ancient uplands. The area was home to possums and other small mammals, too. And in the lakes and rivers, there were turtles and crocodiles. One river animal, called *Champsosaurus* (CHAMP-so-SORE-us), hunted for gars, sturgeons, rays, and other kinds of fish.

There were lots of insects similar to those we are familiar with, including beetles and flies. *Leptoceratops* might even have been bothered by biting flies in the rainy season.

In the air, *Leptoceratops* would have seen a few birds, but they were mostly shore birds and water birds, not song birds like those we see today. The biggest flying animals were pterosaurs (TERR-o-sores), like *Pteranodon* (Terr-AN-o-don). There were no bats at night, because bats had not evolved yet.

Dinosaur Neighbors

Other dinosaurs also lived near *Leptoceratops*. Many were plant eaters, and all of them were bigger than *Leptoceratops*. *Alamosaurus* (AL-a-mo-SORE-us) was the only long-necked plant eater around. *Ankylosaurus* (An-KYE-low-SORE-us) was the biggest of the armored dinosaurs. *Edmontosaurus* (Ed-MONT-o-SORE-us) was a duck-billed dinosaur. *Torosaurus* (TORE-o-SORE-us) was a horned dinosaur with a huge head. And *Triceratops* (Try-SERR-a-tops) was the biggest horned dinosaur of them all.

Corythosaurus

Edmontosaurus

Brachiosaurus

Probably none of the plant eaters fought with *Leptoceratops*, but they might have kept it away from the best plants. After all, they were all bigger and stronger.

There were also meat-eating dinosaurs. The biggest was *Tyrannosaurus* (Tye-RAN-o-SORE-us), which was forty-three feet (thirteen meters) long, and as heavy as a big elephant. *Albertosaurus* (Al-BURT-o-SORE-us) also lived near *Leptoceratops,* and a big *Albertosaurus* was twenty-seven feet (eight meters) long. If either of these predators saw *Leptoceratops, Leptoceratops* would have to hide in the bushes or run like crazy.

Ankylosaurus

Triceratops

Life of Leptoceratops

A baby *Leptoceratops* was probably about the size of a kitten. Dinosaurs grew quickly, and it would have taken a baby *Leptoceratops* only a few years to become an adult. Throughout its life, it probably lived in a herd with other *Leptoceratops*.

When *Leptoceratops* grew up, it began to look for a mate. Male *Leptoceratops* probably fought with each other to impress the females, the way many horned animals do today. But since their horns were small, the worst they could do was bang their heads together, or poke at each other with their noses and feet.

Female *Leptoceratops* dug nests and laid their eggs in them. We don't know whether *Leptoceratops* mothers looked after the nests, or whether the fathers helped. It is possible that adults simply went away and left the eggs to hatch.

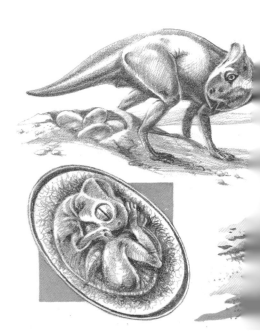

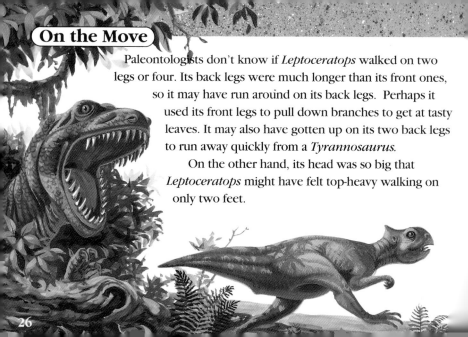

On the Move

Paleontologists don't know if *Leptoceratops* walked on two legs or four. Its back legs were much longer than its front ones, so it may have run around on its back legs. Perhaps it used its front legs to pull down branches to get at tasty leaves. It may also have gotten up on its two back legs to run away quickly from a *Tyrannosaurus*.

On the other hand, its head was so big that *Leptoceratops* might have felt top-heavy walking on only two feet.

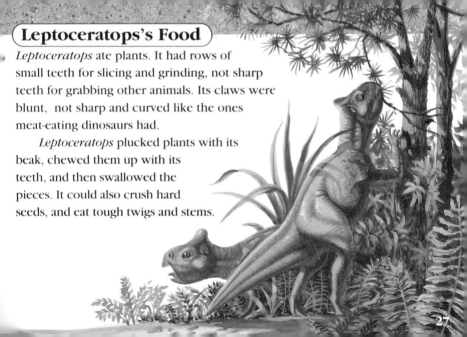

Leptoceratops's Food

Leptoceratops ate plants. It had rows of small teeth for slicing and grinding, not sharp teeth for grabbing other animals. Its claws were blunt, not sharp and curved like the ones meat-eating dinosaurs had.

Leptoceratops plucked plants with its beak, chewed them up with its teeth, and then swallowed the pieces. It could also crush hard seeds, and eat tough twigs and stems.

Why Dinosaurs Became Extinct

Dinosaurs roamed the earth for 160 million years. Then about 65 million years ago, a strange thing happened. All the dinosaurs died off. Many other animals also became extinct at the same time. All the flying reptile pterosaurs died off. All the big reptiles in the sea died off, too, except for crocodiles. And many mammals died off.

There are hundreds of different theories to explain why they all disappeared. One theory says the climate changed, and the plants changed, too.

This theory was invented by paleontologists who study fossil plant leaves. They say that dinosaurs died off because they weren't able to change with the climate.

There is another theory based on the rocks that were formed when dinosaurs became extinct. Scientists who study these rocks think that either a big meteorite struck the earth, or that many big volcanoes erupted, causing a lot of dust to be sent up into the air.

Dinosaurs probably became extinct after a big meteorite hit the earth. The dust sent into the air would have blotted out the sunlight. Plants would have had a hard time growing. This situation may have lasted for many months or many years. In that time, all the dinosaurs would have starved to death.

Farewell to Leptoceratops

Leptoceratops was only one of many hundreds of kinds of dinosaurs, but it was one of the most interesting. Of all the horned dinosaurs that lived in North America, it was the smallest and had a bump on its nose. It could walk on either two legs or four. Some dinosaurs are known from only a few bones, but several good fossil skeletons of *Leptoceratops* have been discovered.

Leptoceratops was one of the last dinosaurs to live. Most other kinds of dinosaurs had become extinct long before it evolved. *Leptoceratops* is part of the mystery of what killed the last dinosaurs.

Perhaps there is a fossil that will provide a clue. Perhaps you will be the one to find it.